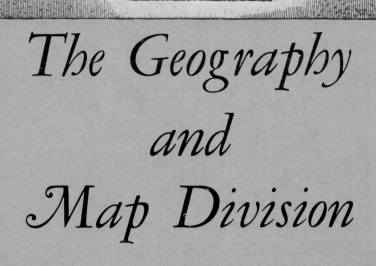

The Geography
and
Map Division

GUIDE TO ITS COLLECTIONS AND SERVICES

The Geography and Map Division

A GUIDE TO ITS COLLECTIONS AND SERVICES

Revised Edition

U.S. LIBRARY OF CONGRESS   WASHINGTON   1975

COVER: *During the late 16th and the early decades of the 17th centuries, a number of navigation atlases were published in the Netherlands, in Dutch, English, and French editions. The nautical scene on the cover is the frontispice in the 1622 edition of Willem Janszoon Blaeu's* The Light of Navigation.

FRONTISPIECE: *This decorative compass rose illustrates the introductory geographical description in volume one of Blaeu's 12-volume* Le Grand Atlas, *1667, one of the most magnificent atlases ever published.*

LIBRARY OF CONGRESS CATALOGING IN PUBLICATION DATA

United States. Library of Congress. Geography and
  Map Division.
  The Geography and Map Division.

  Edition for 1951 issued by the Map Division under
title: The services and collectives of the Map Division.
  1. United States. Library of Congress. Geography
and Map Division. I. United States. Library of
Congress. Map Division. The services and collections
of Map Division. II. Title.
Z733.U63G46 1975   026'.912   74-30313
ISBN 0-8444-0150-1

For sale by the Superintendent of Documents, U.S. Government Printing Office
Washington, D.C. 20402 - Price $1.15
Stock Number 3004–00015

Preface

MAPS ARE EPHEMERAL and transitory things. Because currency and accuracy are among their most valued attributes, they have high incidences of attrition and obsolescence. The life expectancy for most maps, in fact, is intentionally brief.

Consider, for example, the 200 million or more road maps which were acquired by motorists during the past 12 months. Many of these maps are already outdated and will soon be superseded by new, revised editions. The vast majority of last year's road maps are already destined for the paper baler or incinerator. By the end of this year perhaps fewer than 20,000 of the original 200 million road maps will have survived. Within five years there may be under 1,000 extant copies.

Road maps, it is true, are among the most temporal of the cartographer's products. But impermanence is a peculiarity of most maps and charts. For navigating on the seas or through the air, use of an obsolete chart may be not only foolhardy but downright dangerous.

Because of the high premium placed on their currency, the physical vulnerability of most cartographic formats, and the reluctance of many librarians and curators to regard them as legitimate objects to collect and preserve, maps are among the rarest documentary records. Nonetheless, substantial numbers of maps and charts have been preserved in archives, libraries, and museums throughout the world, as well as in private collections. In the United States, as in most foreign countries, the largest cartographic collections are under official custody. There are, however, also within this country at least 35 college, university, public, and society libraries with collections of more than 100,000 maps.

Admittedly, few maps are made for posterity. Most of them, however, have value historically to document conditions for a specific place at a given time. It is essential, therefore, that cartographic records be collected and preserved along with other historical materials.

Navigating with obsolete hydrographic charts, as noted previously, is hazardous. A sequence of such outdated charts, however, is invaluable in studying shoreline changes over a period of years, Similarly, automobile road maps published half a century ago are of little use to today's motorists. The annual editions of road maps issued by automobile associations, oil companies, and state highway departments over the past 60 years, however, provide the best records for studying the development and expansion of the highway network of the United States.

As we prepare to celebrate the bicentennials of the Revolutionary War and the founding of our Republic, contemporary maps of the late 18th century are in increasing demand by historians, writers, and administrators. The centennial of the Civil War, a decade ago, similarly stimulated interest in maps of the 1860's.

More personal interests in maps include examination of 19th-century county maps and atlases for genealogical research to locate names and land holdings of ancestors. Reproductions of historic maps preserved in libraries are also valued as wall hangings, particularly when they depict areas which have a personal or ancestral interest to the owner.

Although map collecting and preservation have become accepted responsibilities of libraries and archives only during the past century, the reasons for collecting cartographic records were recognized more than four centuries ago. In the preface to the *English Euclid,* published in 1570, Dr. John Dee wrote:

> Some to beautify their Halls, Parlers, Chambers, Galeries, Studies, or Libraries with; other some, for things past, as battles fought, earthquakes, heavenly firings, and such occurrences, in histories mentioned: thereby lively as it were to view the place, the region adjoining, the distance from us, and such other circumstances: some other, presently to view the large dominion of the Turk: the wide Empire of the Muscovite: and the little morcel of ground where Christiandom (by profession) is certainly known, little I say in respect of the rest, etc.: some other for their own journeys directing into far lands, or to understand other.men's travels . . . liketh, loveth, getteth and useth Maps, Charts, and Geographical Globes.

More prosaically, it is important for libraries to collect maps today because they may be expected to appreciate greatly in value in the years ahead. Thus, a first edition of Abraham Ortelius' *Theatrum Orbis Terrarum,* 1570, purchased for the Library in 1908 for less than $500 by Philip Lee Phillips, first chief of the Map Division, has a current estimated value of 40 or 50 times that figure. Numerous other cartographic items acquired six or more decades ago have likewise appreciated greatly in monetary as well as intrinsic value.

In 1951 the Library of Congress published a small monograph entitled *The Services and Collections of the Map Division.* During the more than two decades that have passed since that first guide was published, the division has been redesignated the Geography and Map Division, the cartographic collections have expanded by more than 40 percent, computerized cataloging procedures have been developed and utilized, a number of publications have been issued, 24 successive summer special map processing projects have been sponsored, and the division has been relocated to temporary, leased quarters in suburban Alexandria, Va. The current holdings of the division, its organization and functions, and the reference services it offers are detailed in this revised and enlarged guide.

Walter W. Ristow, *Chief*
Geography and Map Division

Contents

iii   Preface

1   Introduction

8   The Collections

10   Special Collections

     10   Discovery and Exploration Periods

     16   Colonial America, the French and Indian War, and the American Revolution

     21   Post-Revolutionary War Period

     24   Pre-Civil War Period

     24   Civil War Maps

     27   Post-Civil War Period

     29   United States Official Maps and Charts

     30   Foreign Military, Topographic, Cadastral, and Hydrographic Surveys

     31   Oriental Map Collection

     33   Atlases

     35   Globes

39   Organization and Services

Many 17th and 18th century atlases include astronomical charts and tables and representations of scientific instruments, globes, and armillary spheres. The armillary sphere reproduced here illustrates Claude Buy de Mornas' Atlas méthodique et elémentaire de géographie et d'histoire, *published in 1761.*

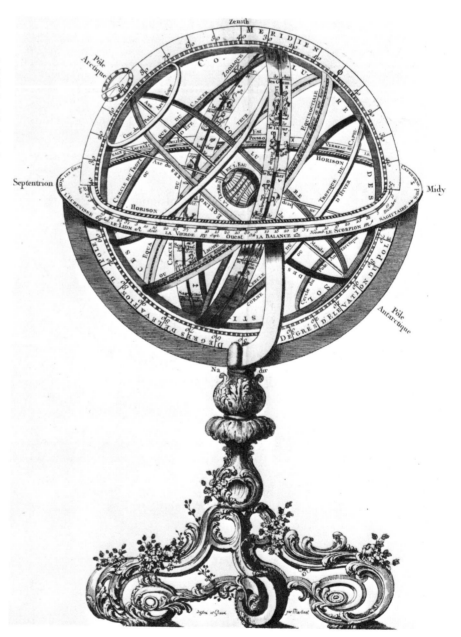

Introduction

A HALL OF MAPS AND CHARTS was one of several new administrative and custodial units established when the Main Building of the Library of Congress was opened in November 1897. The official designation of the cartographic unit evolved during the next three-quarters of a century successively to Maps and Charts Department, Division of Maps and Charts, Division of Maps, Map Division, and, most recently, in 1965, Geography and Map Division. Similarly, as the collections expanded the division was periodically relocated, initially within the Main Building, following World War II to the Annex Building, and in October 1969 to leased quarters in suburban Alexandria, Va., some 12 miles from the Main and Annex Buildings. The division is scheduled to return to Capitol Hill upon completion of the Library's James Madison Memorial Building.

Although administratively the history of the Geography and Map Division covers but three-quarters of a century, the holdings of the Library of Congress, at its establishment in 1800, included three maps and four atlases. The cartographic collections had expanded to seven maps and six atlases when the first *Catalogue of Books, Maps and Charts Belonging to the Library of the Two Houses of Congress* was published in April 1802. A decade later the Library possessed some 50 maps and an unrecorded number of atlases. These and most of the other holdings of the Library were destroyed in 1814, when British soldiers burned the Capitol.

To reconstitute the Library, Thomas Jefferson offered his personal collection of books and other reference materials, which he had carefully and selectively assembled over a period of 50 years. Fortunately, the Congress approved the purchase of this private scholarly library, and the materials were transported from Monticello to Washington in horse-drawn wagons in the spring of 1815. Geography was one of the intellectual interests of the well-read Jefferson, and a number of general and regional geographical books, as well as a rich selection of atlases and maps, were included in the acquisition. Many of these items are described in volume four of the five-volume *Catalogue of the Library of Thomas Jefferson,* which was compiled, with annotations, by E. Millicent Sowerby and published by the Library of Congress (1952–59).

During the next several decades additional cartographical items were acquired by purchase, gift, exchange, and official deposit. There is no record of the size of the map and atlas collections on December 24, 1851, when fire swept through the Library's rooms in the Capitol.

The official report on the conflagration, issued on January 7, 1852, indicated that some 35,000 books were destroyed as well as "nearly all our extensive collection of Maps." The collections were once again reconstituted, but without the nucleus of a Jefferson library. Maps and atlases, published in greater numbers after the middle of the 19th century, were among routine acquisitions.

During the 1850's, three unofficial proposals to establish a separate map department in the Library were advanced. The first was made by Lt. Edward B. Hunt at the annual meeting of the American Association for the Advancement of Science, held in Cleveland from July 28 to August 2, 1853. Lieutenant Hunt, who was then on detail to the U.S. Coast Survey, complained that "no [map] collection exists in our land which furnishes full materials for extensive investigations, such as are now more and more demanded by questions of history, science, commerce, and policy." He proposed, therefore, that there be established, preferably at the Libary of Congress, "a complete and special geographical library, . . . [which] would be a valuable aid to all . . . researchers." Because of the difficulties he experienced in conducting his personal research, Lieutenant Hunt further stressed the need "to arrange complete and systematic indexes and catalogs, which would at once make known all the materials so arranged as best to facilitate special research."

Johann Georg Kohl, an eminent German geographer and Americanist, reiterated two years later the need for a systematic cartographic collection. His "Substance of a Lecture delivered at the Smithsonian Institution on a Collection of Charts and Maps of America," was published in the 1857 annual report of the Smithsonian.

Prof. Daniel Coit Gilman of Yale University included a plea for a federal map collection in an article entitled "The Last Ten Years of Geographical Work in this Country," published in the *Journal of the American Geographical Society* (vol. 3, 1872, p. 111–113). Gilman acknowledged that "many able officers of the government [were] engaged in investigations of the highest value to mankind, [but] much of their usefulness is impaired by the defective arrangements for gathering up, presenting and distributing to the public the results thus ascertained. They likewise point to the importance," Gilman continued, "of having established in Washington, or elsewhere, as a department of the general government, a bureau of maps and charts and geographical memoirs, where all these vast accumulations may be stored, classified and rendered accessible, like the books in the library of Congress . . . so that persons who have the right may make inquiry respecting them."

Regrettably, the successive recommendations of Hunt, Kohl, and Gilman were not acted upon, and several more decades passed before a separate map department was established in the Library of Congress. Nonetheless, during these years the cartographic collections of the Library continued to be augmented through various acquisitions. The volume of accessions, in all formats, increased greatly following passage of the copyright act in 1870, which required mandatory deposit in the Library of Congress of two copies of all copyrighted publications.

Several noteworthy collections of maps were acquired by purchase before 1897. The earliest such accession was the Faden Collection which includes 101 manuscript and printed maps relating to the French and Indian War and the American Revolution. The maps, many of which were drawn by British military engineers, had formed part of the working collection of William Faden, foremost English map publisher during the last quarter of the 18th century. A special congressional appropriation of $1,000 was voted on July 2, 1864, to purchase the Faden Collection from Edward Everett Hale.

In 1867 the Congress purchased for the Library, at a cost of $100,000, the notable collection which had been assembled by Peter Force, distinguished archivist and Americanist. In addition to extensive and valuable holdings of books, pamphlets, manuscripts, journals, and newspapers, the Force purchase included more than 1,200 maps and views. The maps greatly enriched the Library's cartographic holdings. After more than a century of collecting and growth, Force items are still among the rarest treasures in the map collections.

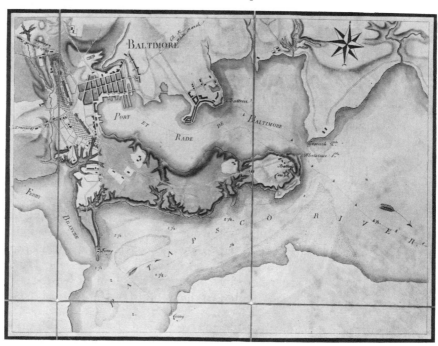

This 1781 map of Baltimore is no. 13 in the Rochambeau Collection of Revolutionary War maps. The original is beautifully colored.

A manuscript atlas and 67 maps were included in the Rochambeau Collection, which was purchased by the Library in 1883 from the Marquis de Rochambeau. These cartographic materials relate to the French land and naval operations in America during the Revolutionary War.

Before the establishment of federal mapping agencies, maps prepared under official authorization were included as supplements in published

3

congressional document series. The maps were printed on contract by various engravers and lithographers. In 1843 some 150 congressional series maps were assembled and bound in a large folio volume, now in the Geography and Map Division. Although an inscription states that "this is not a complete collection of maps, charts &c, published by order of Congress," the volume provides an excellent cross section of United States official mapping over a period of more than two decades.

In 1875 a young man named Philip Lee Phillips joined the staff of the Library of Congress as a cataloger. The youngest son of a prominent Washington, D.C., lawyer and one-time member of Congress, Phillips had been enrolled briefly as a student at Columbian College of Law but had displayed little interest in legal studies. The elder Phillips arranged for him to work at the Library of Congress and, in fact, for almost four years supplied the funds to pay his salary.

Phillips' duties apparently included servicing books and general maintenance of the collections, in addition to cataloging. Early in his career he became painfully aware of the disorganized state of the Library's cartographic materials. In such time that he could spare from his regular duties, Phillips began to organize and catalog the Library's maps and atlases. Because of these efforts and his growing knowledge of maps, their history, and their makers, Phillips came to be recognized as the cartographic specialist. By the time the Library's new building opened in 1897, he had compiled an extensive *List of Maps of America in the Library of Congress,* which was published in 1901. The volume also included a comprehensive bibliography on the literature of cartography. These evidences of his specialized interest and knowledge strengthened Phillips' candidacy for the position of superintendent of the newly created Hall of Maps and Charts, to which he was appointed in 1897.

After the maps were transferred from the Library's rooms in the Capitol to the new building, Phillips estimated that the collection included 47,000 maps and almost 1,200 atlases. The new superintendent initiated various projects to stimulate accessions. In 1902, for example, he sent letters of solicitation to postmasters in the administrative cities of some 2,867 counties. The same year he wrote to official mapping agencies in various foreign countries requesting that their publications be deposited in the Library of Congress on a regular basis.

A year later he recommended to the Librarian "that permanent special agents, whose interest and experiences qualify them, shall be retained to look out and report on the latest map publications in Europe and in South and Central America. An ordinary agent or bookseller is not satisfactory. A cartographer or map dealer who will not only act as agent but as a bureau of cartographical information is needed. Map publications, even when issued for governments, frequently escape our attention for a time, because so little is published concerning maps. An agent such as recommended should make use of

RESIDENCE AND LAW OFFICE OF E.S.GOLDEN, KITTANNING, PENN'A.

BARNET FARM ALDERNEYS. SHORT HORNS.
PROPERTY OF DR T.H.ALLISON
KITTANNING, ARMSTRONG CO. PA.

POTTERFIELD FARM HOLSTEIN CATTLE
OWNED BY
DR. T.H. ALLISON, KITTANNING PENNA.

his business not only to execute orders, but to keep the Division informed on matters relating to cartography." There is no evidence that this recommendation was heeded. Some 40 years later, however, the Library's Map Division, in cooperation with various federal mapping agencies and libraries, established a cooperative foreign map procurement program along the lines proposed by Phillips.

During Phillips' tenure, the cartographic collections were also augmented by transfers of noncurrent maps and atlases from various federal libraries. Of particular note is a large collection of 19th-century county maps and atlases which were transferred by the Coast and Geodetic Survey in 1900. Phillips was also instrumental in acquiring a large number of sheets of large- and medium-scale map series published by Great Britain's Ordnance Survey.

In 1919 the Coast and Geodetic Survey transferred to the Library the original manuscript plan of Washington, D.C., which was prepared by Pierre Charles L'Enfant in 1791. The L'Enfant Plan is valued as one of the most distinctive items in the collections. It is drawn on two sheets which are joined to form a map that measures 28 by 40 inches. The L'Enfant Plan had through the years become badly stained and faded. It underwent a major restoration in 1951, but the map outlines are still very faint. In 1887 the Coast and Geodetic Survey prepared a reproduction from a tracing of the original Plan, which is available at $1.50 a copy from National Ocean Survey, Rockville, Md. 20852.

Phillips' greatest efforts in the Library's cartographic acquisitions program were concerned with increasing the holdings of rare maps and atlases. To achieve this goal he maintained contacts with major European dealers in out-of-print publications. In 1907, 1908, and 1909 he made summer trips to Europe, at his own expense, for the purpose of visiting antique dealers and bookshops. On these expeditions he purchased for the Library's collections many distinctive items at prices which represent but a minute fraction of their present monetary value.

During his entire professional career, Philip Lee Phillips' interests were primarily American and antiquarian, and this is reflected in the Library's early cartographic acquisitions. He was, in short, more concerned with quality than quantity. In his 1907 report, for example, he noted that "while the accessions show an extensive increase in number, the value of the material is not as great as in former years, especially the last year as the opportunity offered of gathering material was helped considerably by a trip to Europe. The Map Division, from its collection and recent accessions," Phillips observed, "is reaching that condition of completeness when only very rare material is needed." Notwithstanding this emphasis on rare and historic accessions, the division's holdings in 1924, the year of Phillips' death, included 170,000 maps and 5,900 atlases, representing gains of 360 and 500 percent, respectively, during Phillips' incumbency.

Phillips' successor, Col. Lawrence Martin, was a professional geographer, with specializations in the physical and military aspects of the discipline. Martin's personal interests were in boundary studies and political geography, and he was also seriously concerned with strengthening the Library's holdings of official set and series maps. Martin's experiences in World War I had introduced him to European map series, many of which he subsequently acquired for the Library. He also established contacts with officials in United States mapping agencies and greatly increased the influx of maps and charts from these sources. Martin's studies of boundaries and of several maps utilized in international treaties stimulated an interest in historical maps. This was reflected in successful projects to obtain photocopies of manuscript maps relating to America from various European and American libraries and archives.

During World War II all federal mapping agencies, as well as most commercial map publishers, were engaged in preparing military maps and charts. Moreover, distributions of many cartographic publications were rigidly restricted during the war years. These conditions were reflected in decreased accessions in the Map Division from 1940 to 1944.

With victory won, military agencies deposited in the Library of Congress selected issues of World War II maps. Map accessions for fiscal year 1945 accordingly passed 58,000, as compared with 7,700 in 1942. Following V-E Day (May 8, 1945) and V-J Day (September 2, 1945), there was rapid contraction of various wartime offices and agencies. Some map libraries, assembled to support various military and intelligence programs, were deactivated, and the Library's Map Division fell heir to their collections. Large military cartographic libraries weeded their holdings and transferred large quantities of maps and charts to the Library. More than 75,000 sheets were accessioned in fiscal 1947, and additional volumes of transferred material, which could not be processed by the small staff, were stored in the unfinished attic of the Annex Building.

Wartime demands had revealed significant gaps in the division's cartographic holdings, particularly in large- and medium-scale foreign topographic series. With the objectives of filling such gaps and reestablishing and expanding foreign exchanges, the Map Division joined with the Department of State and other federal cartographic agencies and libraries to establish a cooperative foreign map procurement program. The Interagency Map and Publication Acquisitions Committee, organized in 1946, is still functioning. The cartographic acquisitions program, coordinated through the Department of State's Office of Map and Publication Procurement, supports geographic attachés in several American embassies, as well as a number of Washington-based cartographic specialists, who make periodic procurement missions to selected countries. For the past quarter-century more than 90 percent of the Library's foreign cartographic accessions, both exchanges and purchases, have come via IMPAC channels.

The Collections

THE GEOGRAPHY AND MAP DIVISION has custody of the world's largest and most comprehensive cartographic collection, which includes more than 3½ million maps and charts, 38,000 atlases, 250 globes, and some 500 three-dimensional relief models. The collections are comprehensive in area, subject, and date, and are particularly rich in Americana. Among the earliest original manuscript maps are three portolan atlases and 17 portolan charts drawn on vellum by Italian, Portuguese, Spanish, and English cartographers in the 15th, 16th, 17th, and 18th centuries. The excellent collection of atlases dates from the earliest printed editions of Ptolemy's *Geography* (1482), which includes maps, and contains representative volumes of all significant publishers of atlases of the last five centuries. There are atlases of individual continents, countries, states, counties, and cities, as well as of the entire world. In addition to general reference atlases, there are works which focus on a wide range of special subjects. Of particular interest to genealogists and local historians is a large collection of U.S. county and state atlases published in the last half of the 19th century. Another noteworthy group includes national, regional, state, and provincial resource atlases published during the past four or five decades. Of particular interest is the *National Atlas of the United States of America,* a 1970 publication of the United States Geological Survey.

The collections also include a number of manuscript and printed maps of colonial America, the Revolutionary War, the War of 1812, the Civil War, and the wars of the 20th century. Supplementing the original historical records are photoreproductions of manuscript maps in various American and European archives.

Approximately 55 percent of the 3½ million maps are individual sheets of large- and medium-scale set maps and charts published during the 19th and 20th centuries. Included are official topographic, geologic, soil, mineral, and resource maps and nautical and aeronautical charts for most countries of the world. The collection of more than a million and a half single-sheet maps includes general and special subject maps of the world and its various geographical and political entities, divisions, and subdivisions. Especially well represented are maps of the United States and each of the 50 states, including numerous county maps and city and town plans. The collection of some 750,000 large-scale fire insurance plans, in bound and loose-sheet series, includes more than 12,000 United States cities and towns. Between 1852 and 1961 as many as seven different editions and revisions for some cities were issued by the Sanborn Map Company and predecessor publishers.

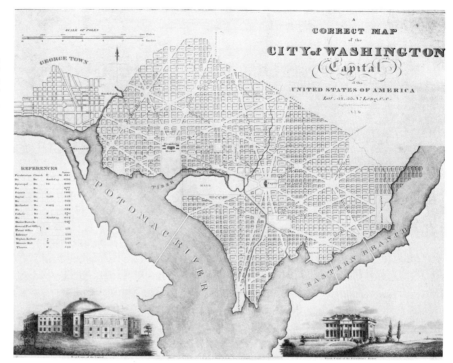

This map of Washington, D.C., copyrighted by Peter Force on January 31, 1820, illustrated annual editions of the National Calendar, *which he published between 1820 and 1836.*

The fire insurance map collection is a unique and detailed cartographic and historic record of America's urban development and growth over more than a century. It was described by Walter W. Ristow in the July 1968 *Quarterly Journal of the Library of Congress* in an article entitled "United States Fire Insurance and Underwriters Maps, 1852-1968."

Special Collections

MOST OF THE MAPS, charts, and atlases in the Geography and Map Division are in the general cartographic collections. Some of the more distinctive and valuable holdings are preserved in a large, 5,000-square-foot masonry vault, which is equipped with independent temperature and humidity controls. Among treasures in the vault are a number of cartographic groups which are maintained as special collections.

Discovery and Exploration Periods

The Kohl and Lowery Collections and the Harrisse bequest are primarily concerned with the discovery and exploration periods of American history. Henry Harrisse (1829-1910) bequeathed to the Library of Congress in 1915 more than 600 tracings and pencil sketches of old maps relating to the discovery and exploration of America, as well as 14 rare manuscript maps. The tracings and pencil sketches were prepared by Harrisse when he was compiling his *Bibliotheca Americana Vetustissima,* originally published in New York in 1866. This noteworthy reference work, which is subtitled *A Description of Works Relating to America Published Between the Years 1492 and 1551,* was reprinted in 1967 by Argonaut, Inc., of Chicago.

The manuscript maps included in the bequest were part of Harrisse's personal library and include several notable treasures. Most distinctive is Champlain's original manuscript of New England and Nova Scotia,

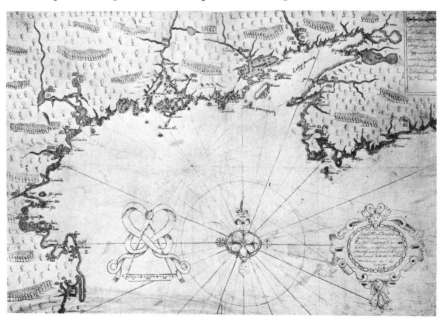

Samuel de Champlain's original manuscript drawing, on vellum, of the coasts of New England and Nova Scotia, 1607, is one of the Library's most distinctive cartographic treasures.

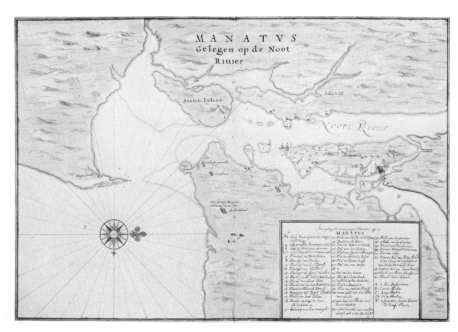

drawn on vellum and dated 1607. It is considered to be the most important of Champlain's large maps. Along the coast are noted, in his own hand, explorations of 1604, 1605, and 1606. Clearly shown on the map is the river which Champlain called St. Croix, as well as Cape Sable and Port Royal. An anonymous vellum map in the Harrisse bequest, entitled "Description dv pais des Hvrons, 1631," is based on one of the very early surveys of the country between Georgian Bay, Lake Simcoe, and Lake Ontario, including the Saugeen Peninsula and part of Lower Ontario. The map may have been made to show the extent and location of established missions. Also in the bequest were manuscript maps of parts of North and South America, drawn in 1639 by Joan Vingboons, cartographer to the Prince of Nassau. Of particular interest is Vingboons' so-called Manatus map of 1639, which is the earliest cartographic representation of Manhattan Island. The maps bequeathed by Harrisse are not maintained as a collection. They are described on cards, under "Champlain" and "Vingboons" in the Geography and Map Division's vault catalog.

No list or catalog has been compiled of Harrisse's sketches and tracings. In the custody of the Rare Book Division are some 220 volumes and pamphlets, as well as several boxes of charts and notes, which also came to the Library with the Harrisse bequest. Information about Harrisse and his bibliographical methods is given in Randolph G. Adams' *Three Americanists* (Philadelphia, 1939) and in Frederick R. Goff's "Henry Harrisse: Americanist" published in the *Inter-American Review of Bibliography* (vol. 3, no. 1, 1953).

The Kohl Collection consists of a series of skillfully executed manuscript copies of maps significant in the history of cartography up to 1834. The 474 maps, with descriptive notes in Kohl's fine hand,

This 1606 survey of Gloucester Harbor in Massachusetts is one of the hand-drawn facsimiles in the Kohl Collection.

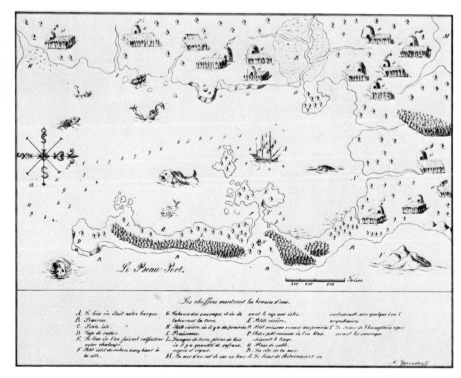

are mounted on acid-free paper backed with muslin. Names, legends, drawings, and symbols are, for the most part, in black ink. On some maps a blue wash has been applied to large rivers and along the coasts. The plates vary considerably in size. The maps were prepared by Johann Georg Kohl, 19th-century German historian, librarian, and Americanist, who brought his valuable collection of maps to the United States in 1854. The U. S. Congress made a grant of $6,000 to Kohl in 1856 to prepare copies of his maps for American scholars as the basis for a catalog of early maps of America. Kohl's drawings were originally deposited in the Department of State but were transferred to the Library of Congress in July 1903. Justin Winsor's detailed description of the collection was published in 1886 by the Harvard University Library as its "Bibliographical Contribution No. 19." Winsor's monograph was reissued by the Library of Congress in 1904 as *The Kohl Collection (now in the Library of Congress) of Maps Relating to America,* with an index by Philip Lee Phillips. Many of the maps, which were so laboriously and carefully handcopied by Kohl, have subsequently been published in facsimile editions. The Kohl copies are, therefore, less in demand today, although his annotations are still of interest and value. The Kohl Collection is briefly described in Walter W. Ristow's "Recent Facsimile Maps and Atlases," in the July 1967 issue of the *Quarterly Journal of the Library of Congress.*

Among other Kohl manuscripts in the custody of the Geography and Map Division are *Chart of the Gulf Stream, Map of the Progress of*

Notes on the Historical Chart
of
the Gulfstream.
from Columbus to Franklin (1770)

1.) On this chart all the dryland is coloured brown. —

2.) The Gulfstream is designated with "pink", being the usually adopted† for hot water. — † colour

3.) To the Gulfstream are given its rough-average limits, and it is traced from the Gulf of Mexico as far as the Azores. —

4.) The cold Eddies along the Western Edge of the G. S., — and the cooler Southeasterly counter-currents on the Eastern Edge are coloured blue. —

5.) The tracks of the old explorers of the G. S. have each their own colour and mark, easily recognizable. —

6.) These tracks are of course only laid down, without entering into details, in their roughest and most probable outlines and direction. —

7.) The small black arrows show the direction of the route, whether out or home voyages. —

8.) Those tracks point out the localities, in which the old navigators entered or crossed the

Discovery of the Gulf of Mexico, and notes and sketches relating to his studies of the U. S. coasts and bordering oceans.

The Lowery Collection was acquired in 1906 through the bequest of Woodbury Lowery, who had made an extensive study of early maps of the Spanish settlements within the present limits of the United States. Lowery's research, carried on over a long period of years, resulted in a two-volume publication on the subject. The list of maps compiled by Lowery includes 740 titles, of which some 300 were in his personal map collection. Approximately 200 additional maps on the list were in the collections of the Map Division in 1906. All but 50 or 60 of the remaining maps on Lowery's original list have subsequently been added to the collection, either as originals or in photoreproductions. In 1912 the Library published *A Descriptive List of Maps of the Spanish Possessions Within the Present Limits of the United States, 1502-1820* by Woodbury Lowery, edited by Philip Lee Phillips.

There are also many individual maps in the collections which have significance for the discovery and exploration periods. A number are described in Clara E. LeGear's "Maps of Early America," published originally in the November 1950 issue of the *Library of Congress Quarterly Journal of Current Acquisitions* and reprinted in *A la Carte, Selected Papers on Maps and Atlases* (Library of Congress, 1972).

Of interest to the early history of Mexico is the "Oztoticpac Lands Map of Texcoco, 1540," a hand-drawn pictorial plan of an Aztec estate in the Valley of Mexico. A detailed study of the map and its significance by the late Howard F. Cline, former director of the Library's Hispanic Foundation, was published in the April 1966 issue of the *Quarterly Journal of the Library of Congress.* Dr. Cline's article has also been reprinted in *A la Carte.*

Among other noteworthy early American maps described in *A la Carte* are Captain John Smith's "Map of Virginia, 1616," Augustine Herrman's "Map of Virginia and Maryland, 1673," and a series of manuscript maps based on boundary surveys made by Spanish commissioners in accordance with provisions of the Treaty of San Ildefonso, signed by Portugal and Spain on October 1, 1777.

Supplementing the original manuscript and printed maps of the discovery and exploration periods are photoreproductions of manuscript maps preserved in various European archives. Of particular note is the Karpinski Collection, which includes photocopies of unique manuscript maps in French, Spanish, and Portuguese archives which bear upon the early history of the American colonies. The 750 photoreproductions were secured through the efforts of the late Louis C. Karpinski, student of cartographical history and one-time professor of mathematics at the University of Michigan. The Karpinski photocopies are not retained as a unit, and the individual maps are filed with the appropriate administrative or geographical units. A list of all the

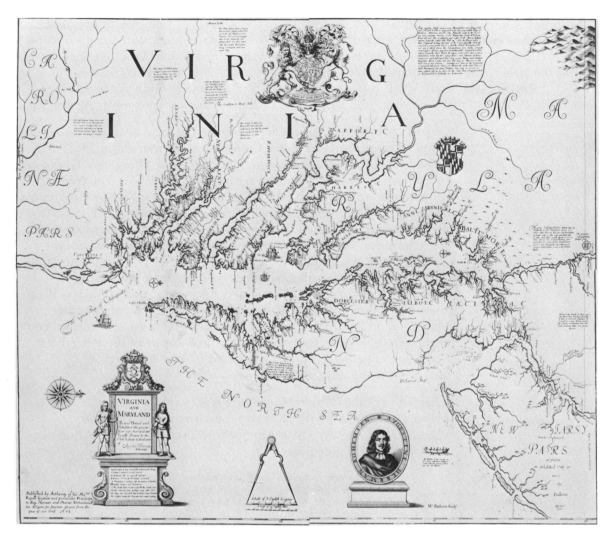

The Library's copy of Augustine Herrman's map Virginia and Maryland *is one of two extant copies in the United States.*

Karpinski reproductions is available for consultation in the Geography and Map Reading Room. Duplicate sets of the Karpinski series are preserved in the William L. Clements, Henry E. Huntington, New York Public, and Newberry Libraries. A note by Dr. Karpinski describing the collection was published in the January 1928 issue of the *American Historical Review*.

Also in the Geography and Map Division are reproductions of manuscript maps relating to North America preserved in the Archivo General de Indias in Seville, Spain. The original maps are described in Pedro Torres Lanzas' *Relacion Descriptiva de los Mapas, Planos, &, de Mexico y Floridas Existentes en el Archivo General de Indias, 1900*.

Colonial America, the French and Indian War, and the American Revolution

The cartographic collections of the Library of Congress, as might be expected, are particularly rich in manuscript and printed maps relating to colonial America and to the French and Indian War and the American Revolution. Pertinent collections, as well as selected individual maps and atlases relating to these periods, are briefly described in LeGear's "Maps of Early America," previously mentioned.

Of particular interest for these periods are the maps acquired with the purchase of the Peter Force Collection of Americana in 1867 (See "The Library of Peter Force," in *The Rare Book Division, a Guide to its Collections and Services,* Library of Congress, 1965.) For years it was suspected that many of the rare historical maps in the Geography and Map Division were acquired with the Force purchase. The Force maps, however, had been dispersed through the general cartographic collections well before establishment of the division, and there was no known list of the original Force maps. In 1970 a reference librarian in the Manuscript Division, while engaged in examining and reorganizing the papers of Peter Force, discovered a list of "Maps, Plans, Views, &c." When the list was spot checked against Geography and Map Division holdings, it became apparent that it was a detailed record of the extensive collection of maps acquired as part of the Peter Force Collection. The Force library is believed to have included at least 1,200 maps and views.

The nature of the cartographic holdings is fairly well documented. Before recommending that Congress purchase the Force library, Librarian of Congress Ainsworth Spofford prepared an evaluation of the materials. He noted that

> . . . in the department of maps and atlases relating to America, the Force library embraces a collection not only large, but in many particulars unique. Not only the early atlases of Delisle, Jefferys, Des Barres, Faden, and other geographers, with a complete copy of the scarce "Atlas of the Battles of the American Revolution," but an assemblage of detached maps over one thousand in number, and chiefly illustrative of America, are here found. Among these, the most valuable are a series of original military plans in manuscript, covering the period of the French war and the war of the Revolution. These are of exceeding interest, and many of them are the work of officers of the British army stationed in America. . . . The number of these original maps, many of which are unpublished and therefore presumed to be unique, is over 300, covering the whole country, from Canada to the Gulf.

Staff members of the division's Reference and Bibliography Section have identified most of the maps on the Peter Force list, and many of these are discussed in "Maps from the Peter Force Collection," by Richard W. Stephenson, published in the July 1973 *Quarterly Journal of the Library of Congress.*

The Seven Years' War and its American extension known as the French and Indian War terminated in 1763. Under the terms of the Treaty of Paris, signed February 10, 1763, England acquired Florida from Spain and all of Canada, as well as that part of Louisiana east of the Mississippi River, from France. For none of these territories were

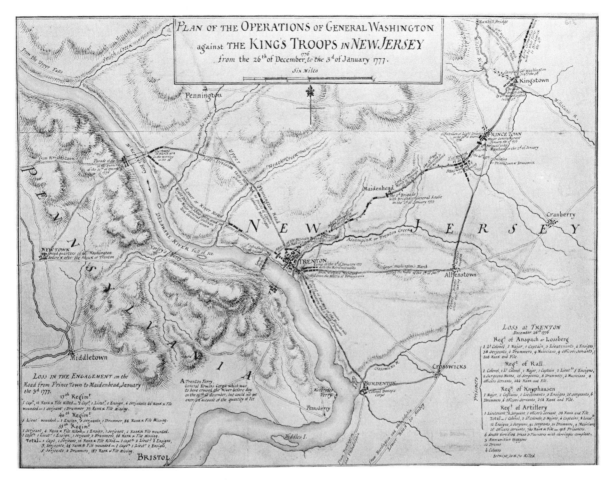

This manuscript map of the Battle of Trenton is from the Faden Collection, which was assembled by William Faden, Geographer to the King of England during the American Revolution period.

there accurate surveys or maps. Accordingly, during the next two decades British military and naval engineers conducted extensive surveys of American lands and waters. Some of the maps were published. Others are preserved in manuscript form in various libraries and archives, among them the Library of Congress Geography and Map Division. Selected items for this period are reviewed in Walter W. Ristow's "Maps of the American Revolution, a Preliminary Survey," published in the July 1971 issue of the *Quarterly Journal of the Library of Congress.* The Library's American Revolution Bicentennial Office, with the cooperation of the Geography and Map Division, plans to compile and publish a list of the Library's maps from the Revolutionary War period.

Several of the Library's more distinctive collections of maps are associated with the French and Indian War and the American Revolution. Brief reference has been made above to the Faden Collection, which was purchased in 1864. The 101 maps and plans, more than half of which are in manuscript form, were assembled by William Faden, geographer to the king of England and foremost British map publisher of the late 18th century. The maps illustrate

17

various aspects of the French and Indian War and the Revolution, with specific reference to the activities of Sir William Howe, and Generals Edward Braddock, John Burgoyne, Henry Clinton, and Charles Cornwallis. Edward Everett Hale, from whom the Library purchased the Faden Collection, describes the collection in his *Catalogue of a Curious and Valuable Collection of Original Maps and Plans of Military Positions Held in the Old French and Military Wars* (Boston, 1862). The Faden maps are also separately cataloged in MARC Map, the Geography and Map Division's computerized map cataloging system.

The Howe Collection was assembled by Adm. Lord Richard Howe, commander of the British fleet in America in 1776 and 1777. It was acquired by the Library in 1905 from members of the Howe family. The 72 manuscript maps and charts, most of which predate the American Revolution, show various parts of the American coast, the West Indies, and the Philippine Islands. Several of the maps may have been consulted by Admiral Howe in naval operations in New York and Philadelphia waters during the Revolutionary War. The Howe Collection maps and charts are cataloged in MARC Map.

The Ozanne Collection consists of 23 sepia-tone manuscript maps and views relating to the operations of the French fleet under Count Charles Hector d'Estaing (1729-92) in the Revolutionary War. They are attributed to Pierre Ozanne because they resemble other works which bear his signature. The maps and views show the French fleet sailing out of the Mediterranean Sea and in various actions along the coast of North America and in the West Indies. Of particular interest are a map and view which depict the siege of Savannah on October 7 and 8, 1779. The Ozanne Collection items, all of which are skillfully and beautifully rendered, are also cataloged in MARC Map.

Brief mention was made previously of the Rochambeau Collection, which was purchased by the Library in 1883. Journals, letters, and papers of the Comte de Rochambeau are preserved in the Library's Manuscript Division. In the Geography and Map Division are 38 manuscript maps carefully drawn by French military engineers, 31 printed maps, and a manuscript atlas with plans of 54 encampments of the French army on its march from Yorktown to Boston, between July 1 and December 2, 1782. The plans are listed separately under entry 1335 in volume 1 of Philip Lee Phillips' *List of Geographical Atlases in the Library of Congress*. Individual manuscript and printed maps in the Rochambeau Collection are also described in MARC Map.

Photocopies of 34 maps in the journals of Comte de Rochambeau were purchased by the Library in 1938 from Rochambeau descendants in Tours, France. They portray French camps on the march from Providence to Williamsburg, June 10 to September 26, 1781. In June 1970 the Library acquired color reproductions of 10 Rochambeau maps from a manuscript atlas entitled *Atlas de la guerre de l'Amerique*, in the collections of the Bibliothèque historique de la Marine, Paris.

Le Vaisseau le Languedoc démâté par le coup de vent dans la nuit du 12. attaqué par un Vaisseau de Guerre Anglois l'apres midy du 13 aoust 1778

Le Languedoc démâté de tous mâts, son Gouvernail en rompû, il a apparaillé deux petites voiles de sa chaloupe pour tacher de diminuer les roulis; mais il ne peut ni avirer ni gouverner; il fait feu de ses cinq Canons & retraite un canon de 36. a été démonté dès la premiere volée de l'ennemi dont les boulets l'enfilent de long en long en perçant le tableau de l'arriere partie la moins forte du Vaisseau vont jusqu'à la Gatte.

Le Renown de cinquante Canons Capitaine Dawson enfilant le Languedoc en le battant de vingt cinq pieces de Canon.

N. 1 Le Lord Howe pendant la chasse avoit quitté son Vaisseau pour la frigate l'Apollon; elle fut aussi démâté pendant le coup de vent.
2 Le Renown cessa de lui même le combat contre le Languedoc, rien ne l'empechoit de le continuer; la soirée fut longue et la nuit tres belle.

Additional Rochambeau manuscript maps are known to be in the collections of Princeton University Library, in the private collection of Paul Mellon in Upperville, Va., and in several official French archives. A number of Rochambeau maps, including some 10 from the Library of Congress collections, are reproduced in *The American Campaigns of Rochambeau's Army 1780, 1781, 1782, 1783,* translated and edited by Howard C. Rice, Jr., and Anne S. K. Brown and published in two volumes by Princeton University Press and Brown University Press, 1972.

The largest group of British headquarters maps in the United States for the Revolutionary War period is preserved in the William L. Clements Library at the University of Michigan. The rich holdings include manuscript papers and maps from the personal collections of Generals Gage and Clinton. The maps are described in several published lists. The Geography and Map Division has photoreproductions of many of the manuscript maps in the Clinton and Gage collections. The activities of the British army in New Jersey under Sir Henry Clinton between 1775 and 1782 are shown in a skillfully drawn set of 20 manuscript maps entitled "A Collection of Plans, etc. in the Province of New Jersey, by John Hills, Assistant Engineer," preserved in the Geography and Map Division.

Gen. George Washington's army had meager cartographic resources. In July 1777 Robert Erskine was commissioned geographer and surveyor-general of the Continental Army. Following Erskine's death in October 1789, Simeon DeWitt succeeded to the offices. The only considerable extant collection of Erskine-DeWitt maps, which were never published, is held in the New-York Historical Society, New York City. Photostatic reproductions of the manuscript maps are on file in the Geography and Map Division. Christopher Colles drew heavily on these maps in compiling *A Survey of the Roads of the United States of America* (1789), of which the Library has two copies.

The American waters during the colonial and Revolutionary War periods were charted in successive editions of several marine atlases. British ships navigated American coastal regions for more than a century with the aid of the *English Pilot, Fourth Book*. First published in London in 1689, this atlas was issued in 37 editions to 1794. The Library has 17 of the known editions. Although the *Fourth Book* continued in use through the Revolutionary War period, it had serious limitations. Many of the charts, for example, were not corrected in new editions despite the availability of later surveys.

The Atlantic Neptune *series of charts and views portray the eastern coast of North America during the American Revolution years.*

Before the conflict terminated, British naval commanders had for their guidance a new series of American coastal charts. The *Atlantic Neptune,* as the series was called, was based principally on surveys conducted from 1764 to 1775 under the direction of Joseph Frederick Wallet Des Barres. In the succeeding decade, Des Barres, with headquarters in London, directed a staff of specialists in compiling charts from the survey data and engraving copper plates to reproduce them. Some 250 charts covering the harbors and coasts between Nova Scotia and Florida were ultimately included in the *Atlantic Neptune.* Charts in the *Neptune* series are generally preserved in bound volumes. Because they were customarily assembled to order for a particular ship's captain, no two extant volumes are identical in content. The Geography and Map Division has 19 *Atlantic Neptune* sets, each comprising from one to three volumes. The division also has a number

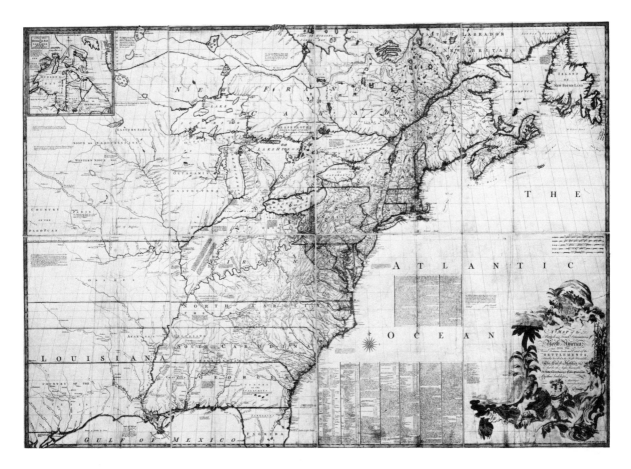

of individual *Neptune* charts as well as four parts of a facsimile edition by Barre Publishers of Barre, Mass.

Also in the cartographic collections are copies of most of the printed maps of America published—principally in Europe—during the 18th century. Of particular note are Henry Popple's *Map of the British Empire in America* (1733), which is represented in three variants and one modern facsimile; Lewis Evans' *General Map of the Middle British Colonies in America* (1755), of which the Library has an unbroken sequence of editions as well as several editions of the descriptive *Analysis* of the map, printed by Benjamin Franklin; and Dr. John Mitchell's *Map of the British and French Dominions in North America* (1755), of which some 20 English, Dutch, French, and Italian variants were published before 1792. An article on John Mitchell and his map, with a table for identifying the various editions, is included in *A la Carte*.

Post-Revolutionary War Period

Most surveying and mapping in English America before and during the Revolutionary War was carried out by British military and naval engineers. Following independence, private and official mapping became American responsibilities. The need for accurate and detailed maps was widespread and urgent. There were, however, no funds to support

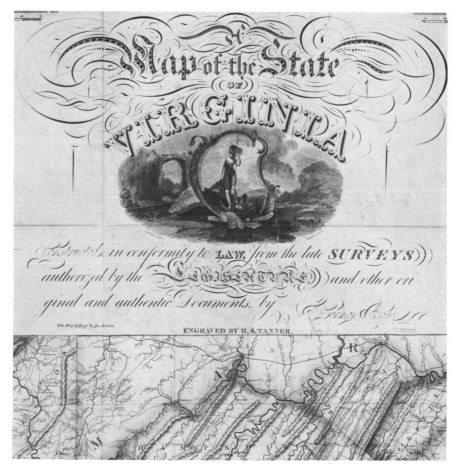

Herman Böÿë's Map of the State of Virginia, 1826, is one of a series of state maps published in the several decades following ratification of the Constitution. Most of the state maps were compiled from county or district surveys prepared by local surveyors.

new surveys and few trained or experienced engineers to conduct them. Maps of the individual states were in particular demand. Because state budgets could not support surveying and mapping programs, concerned citizens took the initiative in preparing maps. They received encouragement and some financial aid from state legislatures. The effectiveness of these efforts is evident from some 30 state maps that were published in one or more editions before 1840. There are in the collections of the Geography and Map Division original, engraved versions or photoreproductions of all the early state maps. The division also has, for several states, photoreproductions of manuscript town and county maps which were used in compiling the maps. Two of the state maps are described in Walter W. Ristow's "Early Maps of Pennsylvania and Virginia," in the July 1966 issue of the *Quarterly Journal of the Library of Congress* and reprinted in *A la Carte.*

In 1925 the Office of Indian Affairs transferred to the Library of Congress a large map of the Missouri River basin, probably prepared by John Evans around 1796, and 12 smaller manuscript maps and sketches. All are believed to have belonged to William Clark and relate to regions of his official activities as superintendent of Indian Affairs. The Evans map has been described as "the most detailed primary

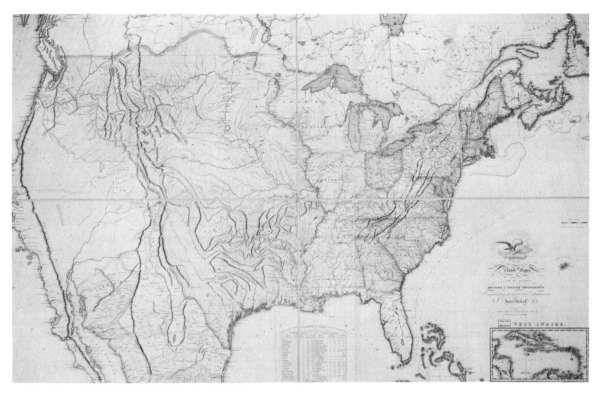

source for geographical knowledge of the Missouri River country that has yet been forthcoming. There is a bare possibility that it was made by or under the direction of Lewis and Clark themselves before they started up the Missouri, being to them a composite itinerary map." (*Geographical Review,* May 1916, p. 329–345) . The Lewis and Clark maps are described in G&M's vault card catalog and were listed in the *Report of the Librarian of Congress* for 1925, p. 84–86.

A number of maps of the United States were published in the first half century or so following ratification of the Constitution. Some were produced in Europe, but American publishers were also active in this field. Most distinguished of the American publishers was John Melish, who, between 1816 and 1823, published no fewer than 24 variants of his *Map of the United States with the Contiguous British and Spanish Possessions.* The Geography and Map Division has copies of all variants in original engravings or photocopies. The map and its variants are discussed in detail in an article entitled "John Melish and His *Map of the United States,*" published in the September 1962 issue of the *Library of Congress Quarterly Journal of Current Acquisitions* and reprinted in 1972 in *A la Carte.*

The Blair Collection is the only group of early 19th-century maps which is maintained as a collection. It includes nine manuscript maps relating to Andrew Jackson's activities in the vicinity of New Orleans and other parts of the Gulf Coast and lower Mississippi Valley. Several of the maps date from the War of 1812, and others bear upon Jackson's postwar activities with the Creek Indians. The Blair Collection of maps was included with the original papers of President Andrew Jackson which were presented to the Library in 1903 by the children of Montgomery Blair, son of Jackson's adopted son, Francis P. Blair. The maps in the Blair Collection are described only in the division's vault card catalog.

Pre-Civil War Period

Surveying and mapping accelerated greatly in the United States in the decades before the Civil War. Favorable cultural, historical, and technological factors stimulated this growth. Between 1810 and 1850, for example, the population of the country tripled. During the same period public land surveys were extended through much of the Middle West, westward movement and settlement were exceedingly active, new states were established, hundreds of miles of roads, canals, and railroads were constructed, and there was an influx of thousands of European immigrants. Particularly significant was the introduction of lithography into the United States, which made it possible to print large runs of maps at low unit cost. In the collections of the Geography and Map Division are examples of some of the earliest maps lithographically reproduced in the United States. Included are cartographic works by William and John Pendleton of Boston, Nathaniel Currier of New York, and Peter Duval of Philadelphia. After 1845, in particular, thousands of state, county, town, city, railroad, and canal maps were published. Numerous town and county land ownership maps were produced during this period, primarily in the New England, Middle Atlantic, and Mid-Western states. The Library's holdings of almost 1,500 county land ownership maps are recorded in Richard W. Stephenson's *Land Ownership Maps, A Checklist of Nineteenth Century United States County Maps in the Library of Congress* (Washington, 1967).

A representative cross section of American cartography during the first half of the 19th century is contained in the Fillmore Collection, which was acquired by the Library in 1916. The maps, some 300 in number, were the personal collection of President Millard Fillmore, and most of the pieces bear his signature. The Fillmore Collection maps have not been individually cataloged.

Civil War Maps

American cartography was only moderately well established when the Civil War broke out. Map coverage was, however, much more extensive for the northern states than for those south of the Mason-Dixon Line. This handicapped both armies during the first year of the war because most of the military operations were conducted in the Confederate States. The Geography and Map Division has rich holdings of Civil War maps in several special collections as well as in the general files. Described in Richard W. Stephenson's *Civil War Maps, an Annotated List of Maps and Atlases in Map Collections of the Library of Congress* (Washington, 1961) are 700 maps, almost all prepared by or for the Union Army. Union maps also predominate in the William T. Sherman Collection, which was assembled by the famous Civil War

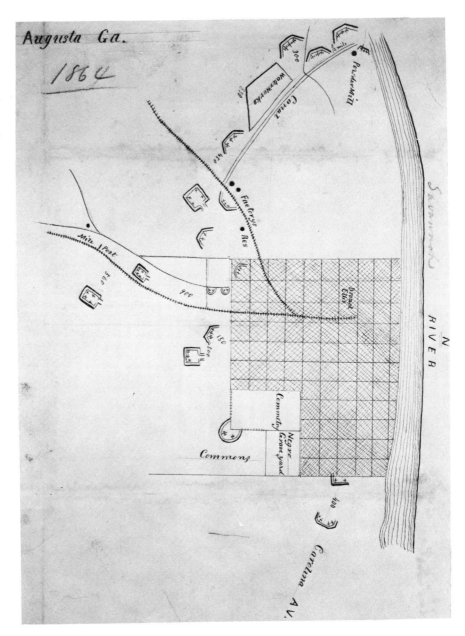

general. There are 179 maps in the collection, 121 of which were acquired on exchange in 1955. The remaining 58 were transferred from the Manuscript Division in 1960. The latter were included in a gift of papers presented to the Library in 1960 by P. T. Sherman of New York City, son of General Sherman. Maps in the Sherman Collection are individually described in the vault catalog. Those which contain military information are also described in *Civil War Maps*.

In 1948 the Library purchased the maps, sketchbooks, journals, correspondence, and personal papers of Maj. Jedediah Hotchkiss, a topographical engineer who was attached, variously, to the staffs of Gen.

25

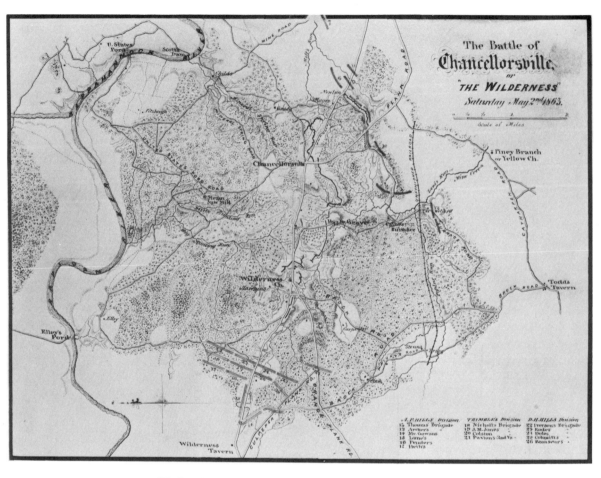

T. J. "Stonewall" Jackson, and other Confederate officers. There are
some 500 maps in the Hotchkiss Collection, of which 340 are
manuscripts relating principally to actions in Virginia and West
Virginia between 1861 and 1863. Hotchkiss' postwar activities in the
development of mines, railroads, and towns are also represented.
Clara E. LeGear's article "The Hotchkiss Collection of Confederate
Maps," published in the November 1948 *Library of Congress Quarterly
Journal of Current Acquisitions*, is reprinted in *A la Carte* (1972).
The Library published in 1951 *The Hotchkiss Map Collection, a List
of Manuscript Maps, Many of the Civil War Period, Prepared by
Maj. Jed Hotchkiss, and Other Manuscript and Annotated Maps in his
Possession,* compiled by Clara E. LeGear, with a foreword by
Willard Webb.

In recent years the Hotchkiss Collection has received several
noteworthy additions. In 1964 Mrs. R. E. Christian, granddaughter of
Major Hotchkiss, presented to the Library a large and detailed
manuscript topographic map of the Shenandoah Valley. It was prepared
by Hotchkiss at the personal request of Gen. T. J. "Stonewall"
Jackson. The collection was again enriched in 1965, when the U.S.
Geological Survey transferred to the Library a manuscript map of

Greene County, Va., which was prepared by Hotchkiss. The map had been lent to the Survey in the 1880's and, inadvertently, was never returned to the distinguished cartographer.

The Geography and Map Division has photoreproductions of another group of Confederate records, the Gilmer-Campbell maps, from originals in the Virginia State Historical Society, Richmond; the United States Military Academy, West Point; and the College of William and Mary, Williamsburg. The maps were made during 1862-64, chiefly under the direction of Maj. Albert V. Campbell, chief of the Topographical Department of the Army of Northern Virginia. Campbell was one of the assistants to Gen. Jeremy F. Gilmer, chief of engineers of the Confederate States of America. The 63 maps are listed in *Library of Congress, Division of Maps, Noteworthy Maps with Charts, Views and Atlases,* compiled by Lawrence Martin (U.S. Government Printing Office, 1927).

Post-Civil War Period	Commercial map publishing expanded greatly after the Civil War because of improved surveying and printing techniques and in response to the greater demand for maps in connection with the exploration and settlement of the west and expansion of the country's rail network. Perfection of color printing, the marriage of photography with lithography, and improvements in high-speed power presses in particular contributed to map production in the last three decades of the 19th century. There was renewed interest in county maps after 1865, as the map men extended their activity to the midwestern states and beyond the Mississippi. There was also some production of maps for counties in the Pacific Coast states. The Library also has extensive holdings of the post-Civil War county maps, most of which are listed in *Land Ownership Maps,* cited above.

Railroad maps and town and city maps were also produced in great numbers during these years. Most of these came to the Library as copyright deposits. A summary by Andrew Modelski of American railroad mapping to the end of the 19th century, as reflected in the Library's collections, was published in the *Proceedings of the American Congress on Surveying and Mapping, 32nd Annual Meeting* (Washington, 1972). A distinctive urban collection consists of the detailed, large-scale fire insurance and underwriters maps prepared for some 12,000 American towns and cities over a period of more than a century, beginning around 1850. Although a number of different publishers produced such maps before 1915, for the subsequent 50 years the Sanborn Map Company enjoyed a virtual monopoly in publishing fire insurance maps. The Geography and Map Division has approximately 750,000 insurance maps in bound and unbound sets. For some sheets there are as many as seven or eight different editions. The insurance map collection constitutes an unexcelled record of urban growth and development in the United States. The Geography and Map Division also has real estate atlases, in various editions, for the larger cities of the country.

After 1870, and continuing into the 20th century, there was a lively interest in producing panoramic or birdseye-view maps of American cities. Although only a small number of artists and mapmakers were involved, they produced within a period of 50 years more than 1,500 panoramic maps of cities and towns. Some 1,200 of these are in the Geography and Map Division. John R. Hébert's article "Panoramic Maps of American Cities" was published in the December 1972 issue of *Special Libraries*. A checklist of the Library's panoramic city maps, compiled by Dr. Hébert, was recently published. It includes, among others, noteworthy groups of panoramic maps prepared by Thaddeus Fowler and Albert Ruger, two of the most prolific panoramic artists.

The Ephraim G. Squier Collection was acquired by the Library in 1909 from Stewart Culin of the Brooklyn Institution of Arts and Sciences Museum. Squier's manuscript field notes are preserved in the Manuscript Division. In the Geography and Map Division are 38 mid-19th-century maps of Central America and Peru which were drawn by Squier, a colorful 19th-century American journalist, diplomat, archeologist, and scholar. The maps were prepared while Squier was

This 1915 map of New York State, issued for the Gulf Refining Company, is one of the earliest oil company road maps. More than 10 billion automobile road maps have been distributed free through gasoline service stations over the past six decades.

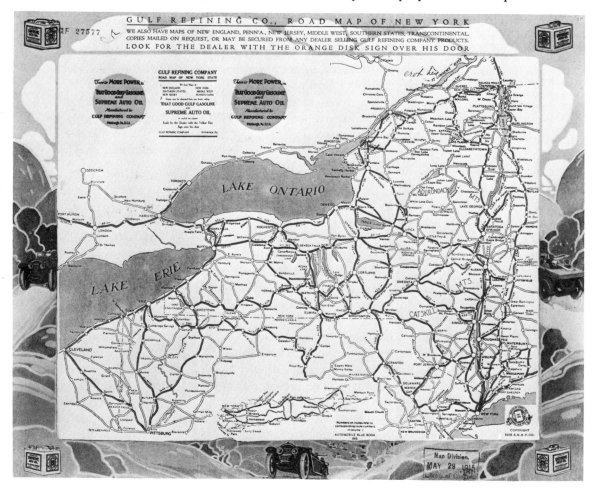

28

engaged in diplomatic and scientific activities in Central America and Peru. They are, for the most part, rough, unfinished pencil and pen-and-ink maps which were drawn from notes and field sketches. Their geographic content is of only incidental importance, and they have significance primarily for the light they shed on United States-Latin American relations in the mid-19th century. The Squier maps are listed and described by John R. Hébert in a paper entitled "Maps by Ephraim George Squier," which was published in the January 1972 *Quarterly Journal of the Library of Congress.*

In 1970 the Manuscript Division transferred to the Geography and Map Division printed official and commercial maps which relate to Gen. John L. Hines' activities on the western front, in Belgium and France, during World War I. There is a list in the Geography and Map Reading Room of the 185 maps in the Gen. John L. Hines Collection.

The Ethel M. Fair Collection includes more than 1,000 pictorial maps, most of which were published in the 20th century. The collection, assembled by Miss Fair over a period of more than four decades, was presented to the Library in 1972. A card catalog, prepared by Miss Fair some years ago and brought up-to-date by G&M personnel, provides access to the individual maps.

A significant and uniquely American cartographic development of the 20th century is the free automobile road map. The Geography and Map Division has annual editions of most of the series distributed by the several large producers of petroleum products, dating back to 1915. Also in the collections are current and retrospective editions of American Automobile Association road maps and annual issues of maps published by official state highway commissions.

United States Official Maps and Charts

Official United States map publishing increased in importance during the latter decades of the 19th century and has greatly accelerated during the present century. Of particular significance was the establishment of the Geological Survey in the Department of the Interior in 1879. The Survey's Topographic Branch has responsibility for compiling and publishing the official topographic map of the United States and for various mineral and resource maps and atlases. Since World War II, most maps in this series have been published at the scale of 1:24,000 (one inch equals 2,000 feet). The Geography and Map Division retains in its collections all editions of the topographic map of the United States and of other official map and chart series.

The Coast and Geodetic Survey was the first established federal surveying and mapping agency. Administratively part of the Department of Commerce, the National Ocean Survey, as it is now known, has responsibility for establishing geodetic controls for the country and for compiling and publishing nautical charts of our coasts and harbors and aeronautical charts of the United States.

There are some 40 additional federal agencies involved in domestic mapping and charting. By law, all deposit their cartographic publications in the Library of Congress. Included are highway maps, soil maps and atlases, mineral and resource maps, irrigation and reclamation maps, navigation charts of the Great Lakes and Mississippi River, and administrative and boundary maps, among others.

The Defense Mapping Agency, established in 1972 by consolidation of former Department of Defense cartographic units, has responsibility for preparing maps and charts of all parts of the world, in the interests of the defense and security of the United States. Its three principal functional units are the Aeronautical Chart and Aerospace Center, the Hydrographic Chart Center, and the Topographic Center. Because of security and other restrictions, there is only selective and limited distribution of maps and charts published by the Defense Mapping Agency.

Foreign Military, Topographic, Cadastral, and Hydrographic Surveys

Largely in response to the need demonstrated by the Napoleonic Wars for larger scale and more accurate maps, major European countries established official surveying and mapping agencies during the first half of the 19th century. By the end of the century the movement had extended to other parts of the world, and official publishers were producing approximately 80 percent of all maps and charts. Some topographic sets of the principal European nations were acquired by the Library before the establishment of a separate Map Division. Additional sets were obtained during the tenure of Philip Lee Phillips.

In 1905 the division published the *Check List of Large Scale Maps Published by Foreign Governments (Great Britain Excepted),* describing the cartographical publications of 31 countries. A separate checklist for Great Britain was contemplated at the time but, regrettably, was never completed. The *Check List,* as stated in the Prefatory Note was compiled "in the hope that when it has been sent to map-publishing bureaus of foreign governments, and to other map distributing agencies, the deficiencies will be noted and both information and maps supplied in order to complete the files of this division." The publication apparently did stimulate further receipts of national cadastral and topographic surveys. As noted above, Phillips' successor, Lawrence Martin, concentrated much of his effort on acquiring foreign large- and medium-scale map series. Future plans of the Geography and Map Division include compiling and publishing lists of these foreign map series.

The Geography and Map Division also has current and retrospective editions of nautical charts, compiled and published by official hydrographic bureaus of various countries. These numbered charts are controlled by means of index maps which accompany the sales catalogs issued periodically by the respective hydrographic bureaus.

Oriental Map Collection

Most of the special cartographic collections in the division are concerned with American maps. Noteworthy exceptions are the early maps of China, Korea, and Japan in the Hummel, Warner, and miscellaneous oriental map collections. In 1930 Andrew W. Mellon, who was at the time secretary of the treasury, purchased for the Library a collection of 38 rare Chinese maps and atlases. The collection had been carefully assembled by the distinguished orientalist Arthur W. Hummel over a period of more than a decade and half, while he was a resident of China. The initial purchase included the following items: two manuscript atlases of all China, each containing 20 maps, drawn in the Ming period (A.D. 1368–1644); an atlas of China, printed before 1662, comprising 20 maps; a large manuscript wall map of China, prepared about 1673; a map of the world, printed in Peking in 1674, by the Jesuit priest Ferdinand Verbiest; two large wall maps of China, one printed in 1821, the other drawn in water color in 1831; a large 18th-century manuscript wall map of South China; a manuscript scroll map of the territory bordering the Great Wall; two mariner's

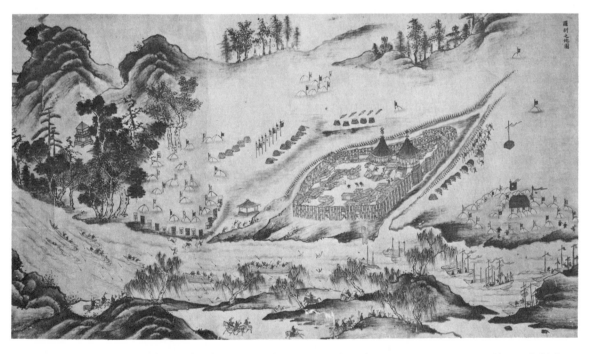

The Hummel Collection includes a number of delicately drawn pictorial Chinese scroll maps.

charts, both manuscript (a scroll and an atlas) of the coastline of China from Tientsin to Canton and beyond; a rare manuscript road map of the great and ancient highway from Sian in Shensi to Ch'engtu in Szechuan Province; an 18th-century manuscript atlas of Chekiang Province; a manuscript atlas of Fukien Province, drawn on satin during the 18th century; an old manuscript wall map of Shantung, Honan, and Chihli Provinces; a detailed manuscript map of the City of Nanking showing how it was captured from the T'aiping rebels in 1864; an old painted map of the Ming Tombs, north of Peking; a manuscript military map of the mountain passes on the southern border of Kuangsi Province; two manuscript military maps of the Yunnan-Szechuan border; a military wall map showing defenses of Kuangsi Province; an 18th-century manuscript map of the city of Hangchow; a wall map of the Ch'ien-t'ang River and the Hangchow bore, made during the 18th century; a wall map of the coast of Chekiang Province in the 18th century; a plan of the city of Lai'chow, Shantung Province; an old manuscript wall map of Kirin Province; a painted wall map of T'aiyuan, the capital of Shansi Province, perhaps 50 to 80 years old; an atlas of the region about Ch'angsha, made during the 18th century; a manuscript atlas of the world of the late 19th century; a printed atlas of Formosa before the Japanese occupancy; and three manuscript maps (two scrolls and an atlas) of the course of the Yellow River.

Dr. Hummel was subsequently appointed chief of the Library's Orientalia Division. While on an official procurement mission to China, in 1934, he purchased for the Geography and Map Division 31 additional early Chinese maps and atlases. In 1962, several years after his retirement from the Library, Dr. Hummel presented to the Geography and Map Division a group of 16 rare manuscript maps from his personal collection. The latter are briefly described in the September 1962 issue of the *Quarterly Journal of the Library of Congress* (p. 186).

In 1929 a number of manuscript maps and atlases of Korea and China were acquired from Mr. Langdon Warner of the Fogg Art Museum, Harvard University. Among the items are an undated manuscript atlas of China (Yu Ti Tsung T'u) showing the 13 provinces and two metropolitan areas at the time it was made; which was probably during the Ming period; an atlas representing China in the Ming period but drawn in 1721 by a Korean scholar named Wön; an undated manuscript atlas of the eight circuits of Korea, probably made in the latter part of the 19th century; an undated atlas of Chyun-Chyong Circuit, Korea, which was probably made between 1800 and 1850; a map of Manchuria, 1733–1858, including an inset plan of the city of Sheng-Ching (Mukden); a map of Chyol-La Circuit, Korea, printed on a fan; a hand-colored, wood-engraved map of Korea, made after 1822; a complete set of maps of the eight circuits of Korea showing locations of villages, roads, and rivers, probably made at the close of the 19th century; a set of seven maps showing the administrative circuits of Korea, also late 19th century; a complete set of maps of the eight administrative circuits of Korea, seemingly made in the early part of the 19th century.

In recent years the Orientalia Division has transferred to the Geography and Map Division an assortment of early Chinese and Japanese maps. Supplementing these and the above-noted maps are a number of distinctive maps which were selected from the division's general collections of oriental maps for preservation in the vault. All Chinese and Korean maps in the above categories have been

Mercator's world Atlas, *published in 1595, introduced the term atlas to identify a systematic collection of maps bound in book format. The Library has two copies of the 1595 Mercator Atlas. In a 1974 catalog, a dealer offered a copy of the* Atlas *for $30,000.*

individually described and entered in G&M's MARC Map system. It is anticipated that a printed catalog of the oriental collections will be published at some future date.

Atlases   Because bound volumes are less subject to wear and tear than separate maps, atlases are important items in any historical cartographical collection. As reported in the introduction, atlases were among the initial holdings of the Library of Congress. They have continued to be noteworthy accessions during the past century and three quarters. There are now more than 38,000 atlases in the Geography and Map Division, and the holdings increase by some 800 volumes each year. Atlases are described in detail, with tables of contents supplied for many volumes, in the *List of Geographical Atlases in the Library of Congress.* Volumes 1–4, published between 1909 and 1920, were compiled by or under the direction of Philip Lee Phillips. Volumes 5, 6, and 7, compiled by Clara Egli LeGear, were published, respectively, in 1958, 1963, and 1973. Mrs. LeGear's *United States Atlases,* published in two volumes in 1950 and 1953, includes holdings of a number of other libraries as well as those of the Library of Congress. *United States Atlases* is particularly useful for its descriptions of state, county, and city atlases published during the last quarter of the 19th century and the early years of the 20th century.

The division's holdings include general world atlases, regional volumes for various continents, states, counties, and cities, and special

33

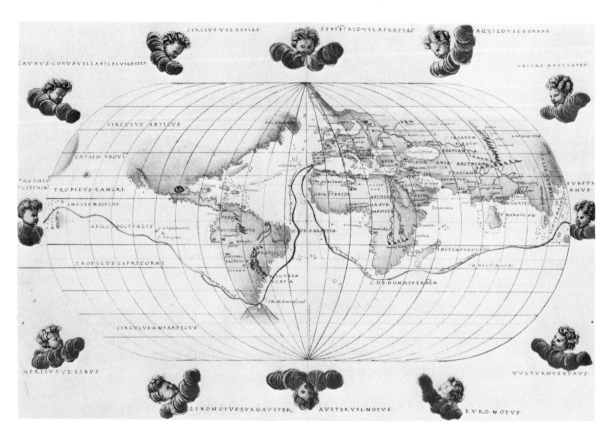

The manuscript atlas of Battista Agnese, produced around 1544, includes 10 colorfully illuminated maps hand-drawn on 15 vellum leaves. Plate 14, reproduced here, shows the world encircled by wind cherubs.

subject or thematic atlases which display historic, economic, physical, climatic, geologic, linguistic, ethnographic, and other mapable data. There are in the collections atlases representative of every period in cartographic history dating from the 15th century. The Library has 45 printed editions (93 copies) of Ptolemy's *Geography* (but no manuscript copies) , and good representation of the various editions of the atlases of Ortelius, Mercator, Blaeu, and other 17th-century publishers.

Publishers of 18th-century atlases represented in the collections include Sanson, D'Anville, Homann, Jefferys, Faden, Moll, Jaillot, Mortier, Senex, Seutter, and Robert de Vaugundy. Atlases of such 19th-century cartographers and publishers as Arrowsmith, John Cary, Laurie and Whittle, Mathew Carey, Pinkerton, Thomson, Vandermaelen, Finley, Brué, Burr, Tanner, Malte-Brun, S. A. Mitchell, C. W. Morse, Colton, and A. K. Johnson are also included. Successive editions of atlases by Bartholomew, Stieler, Andree, Touring Club Italiano, Stanford, Rand McNally, Hammond, and other 20th-century publishers are also represented in the holdings.

34

Several articles in *A la Carte* describe some of the Library's distinctive atlases, i.e., "A Manuscript Atlas by Battista Agnese," "Gerardus Mercator's Atlas of 1595," "Sixteenth-Century Atlases Presented by Melville Eastham," and "Maps of Early America." All originally appeared in issues of the *Quarterly Journal of the Library of Congress*. The Geography and Map Division's outstanding collection of Ortelius atlases is the subject of a paper by Walter W. Ristow entitled "Theatrum Orbis Terrarum, 1570–1970," in the October 1970 issue of the *Quarterly Journal of the Library of Congress*.

In addition to its extensive holdings of original manuscript, engraved, and lithographed atlases, the Geography and Map Division has facsimile editions of a number of rare and historical volumes. Some of the more noteworthy of these are described in "Recent Facsimile Maps and Atlases," in the July 1967 *Quarterly Journal of the Library of Congress*.

Library of Congress printed cards are available for some 60 percent of the atlases in the Geography and Map Division. The remainder are indexed in the *List of Geographical Atlases* and are also recorded in the division's atlas shelflist. All subject cataloging and approximately 60 percent of the descriptive cataloging of atlases is performed in the Geography and Map Division's Processing Section.

Globes The Library has made no concerted effort to assemble a comprehensive collection of globes. There are, nonetheless, some 250 globes in the custody of the Geography and Map Division. They range in diameter from three inches to 50 inches. Over 90 percent are of American manufacture and were made in the 20th or late 19th centuries. The majority were acquired via the Copyright Office. Several distinctive globes warrant brief mention. Most valued is a unique manuscript globe, 72 millimeters in diameter, which was made at Cologne in 1543 by Casper Vöpel (1511-61). The small ball which represents the earth is encircled by 11 adjustable brass rings of an armillary sphere. The Library's Vöpel is one of seven known extant armillary spheres by the German globemaker.

Also in the Geography and Map Division is a set of unmounted globe gores, prepared in 1688 by the celebrated Venetian cartographer Vincenzo Maria Coronelli (1650-1718). The gores were made to fit a sphere approximately 42 inches (110 cm) in diameter. They are reduced copies of a set of gores prepared by Coronelli by order of King Louis XIV of France for a giant globe 15 feet in diameter. A pair of unmounted gores for eight-inch globes, made in 1615 by Jodocus Hondius, are also worth noting. John G. Doppelmeyer's 1755 "Globus terrestris novus" is another distinctive item in the globe collection.

The Library has 13-inch and 3-inch globe pairs (celestial and terrestrial) made by James Wilson of Vermont, first American

Caspar Vöpel's 1543 manuscript globe is the Geography and Map Division's most distinguished example of spherical cartography. The 72-millimeter globe is supported on a brass standard and encircled by an armillary sphere with 11 brass bands.

James Wilson of Vermont was America's first native-born globemaker. This three-inch terrestrial globe, made around 1810, is representative of his earlier works.

globemaker. Wilson began making globes as early as 1810. The Library's three-inch globes are among the earliest he made. The 13-inch globes were made, respectively, in 1831 and 1834.

The largest globe in the Geography and Map Division is 50 inches in diameter. The map for this globe was prepared in the cartographic department of the Office of Strategic Services during World War II. It was mounted on a laminated wood sphere in the globe shops of the Weber-Costello Company, Chicago. Some 12 or 15 copies were made, the first of which went to the office of President Franklin D. Roosevelt and is now preserved in the Roosevelt Memorial Library in Hyde Park, N. Y. Various other allied leaders received copies of the O.S.S. globe, as did the House and Senate Chambers in the U. S. Capitol. The globe in the Geography and Map Division was formerly in the House Chamber.

Three-dimensional relief models have been made and utilized for more than 250 years. Before 1940 most relief models were cast in heavy, fragile plaster, and the attrition rate was great. The Library collections, therefore, include only a limited number of plaster models. During World War II military specifications called for waterproof, wrinkleproof, and tearproof models that could be rolled into compact size, withstand rough handling, and be reproduced in quantity at moderate cost. Models cast in sponge rubber met most of the requirements. They had to be individually handcolored, however, which slowed production and was quite costly.

Following further experimentation, military modelmakers developed three-dimensional molded plastic relief maps for use in the Korean War. A map, in several colors, is printed on a flat sheet of vinyl. The sheet is placed in register on a positive reproduction mold and firmly fastened in the molding press. The plastic sheet is subjected to a high temperature for a period of 10 seconds, after which the map is formed by application of vacuum pressure over the surface of the master mold. During the past quarter century, virtually all three-dimensional maps have been made by this process. Accordingly, plastic maps constitute 95 percent of some 500 relief models in the Geography and Map Division.

Other nonconventional cartographic formats preserved in the division include a hide and driftwood map of the Crown Prince Islands in Disco Bay, Greenland, prepared by a native Eskimo; modern replicas of Marshall Island reed and shell charts; maps printed on cloth; and several oriental ladies' fans decorated with maps. There are also six engraved powder horn maps, four of which date from the French and Indian War and two from the Revolutionary War.

Organization and Services

THE GEOGRAPHY AND MAP DIVISION has a staff of 32, including professionals and nonprofessionals. It is administratively within the Library's Reference Department, but responsibilities and functions span the entire spectrum of library activities. The division is, accordingly, organized in four functional sections, administrative, acquisitions, processing, and reference and bibliography.

The Administrative Section includes the chief, assistant chief, bibliographer, and two secretaries. In addition to directing the activities of the Geography and Map Division, the Administrative Section has immediate management responsibility for the entire Pickett Street Annex Building, which includes three other Library of Congress functional units.

The Acquisitions Section has responsibility for recommending cartographic and geographic items for acquisition by the Library. Coordinating its activities with the Exchange and Gift Division, the section receives cartographic publications through government deposit from various federal, state, and local agencies, via the Copyright Office, and from individual donors. It cooperates with other federal map libraries and mapping agencies on the Interagency Map and Publications Acquisitions Committee to acquire foreign maps and atlases, by exchange or purchase. Personnel in the section also have custody of the division's duplicate files, negotiate piece-for-piece and priced exchanges, and compile and maintain the division's acquisitions statistics and records.

The Geography and Map Division solicits information which may lead to acquisitions. In cooperation with the Library Exchange and Gift Division, it welcomes bequests and gifts of maps and atlases which are not already in the collections. The fair market value of such gifts is tax deductible. Recommendations are regularly made by the Acquisitions Section to the Library's Order Division for the purchase of items offered for sale by dealers or by private individuals.

The Processing Section has custody of the atlas and map collections and is responsible for processing, cataloging, filing, and shelving materials. The MARC Map Unit, established within the Processing Section in 1968, is engaged in cataloging selected maps in machine-readable format. MARC Map is briefly described in Walter W. Ristow and David K. Carrington's "Machine-Readable Map Cataloging in the Library of Congress," in the September 1972 issue of *Special Libraries* (p. 343–352). Although MARC cataloging is currently limited primarily to accessions of new single-sheet and set maps titles, a number of retrospective maps have also been cataloged. As of March 1974, MARC Map storage included more than 26,000 records. In mid-1973 the Library's Card Division began distribution, on a monthly subscription basis, of MARC Map tapes and printed cards.

Maps which have not been individually cataloged are arranged in sequence by administrative area, date, and subject. No catalog card descriptions are available for this material, which includes approximately 45 percent of the map collection.

The Processing Section is also responsible for the care and preservation of the cartographic collections, in cooperation with the Library's Restoration Office. The latter maintains a Map Restoration Shop in the Pickett Street Annex Building. Map preservation techniques include lamination, insertion in transparent mylar envelopes, and wet paste mounting on cloth. Facilities are also available for repairing globes and three-dimensional relief models. The Library's Preservation Research and Testing Office is currently investigating various techniques for mass deacidification. Such treatment is particularly urgent for the large number of 19th- and 20th-century maps and atlases which were printed on highly acid paper.

Since 1951 the Geography and Map Division has sponsored annual summer Special Map Processing Projects, for the purpose of sorting and processing large volumes of noncurrent maps received on transfer from various federal cartographic libraries. Students and university staff members, supported by libraries and geography departments of cooperating colleges and universities, assist permanent Geography and Map Division employees in processing the transfer materials. In exchange for services rendered, cooperative participants select maps and atlases from the division's duplicate collections. In the past 24 summers a million and a quarter duplicates have been selected and distributed to some 90 colleges and universities, and more than 300 individuals have participated in the Special Map Processing Projects.

The Reference and Bibliography Section provides reference service to readers by telephone and in response to mail requests. Limitations on service conform with overall Library of Congress policies and practices. Because the Library functions primarily as a research library, use of the collections is limited to persons of college age and older. High school students are admitted only when access has been requested and justified by the school principal. The division will respond to correspondence inquiries that cannot be serviced by a library in the inquirer's locality. It is not possible, however, to undertake extensive research projects or to assist students in preparing bibliographies, term papers, or other academic assignments. The Geography and Map Division does not lend cartographic materials to individuals. Loans are made to members of Congress and to federal agencies, however, and certain categories of material may be supplied on inter-library loan to research libraries. Individual map sheets, rare maps and atlases, unbound serials, and volumes from the reference shelves are normally excluded from such loan arrangements. Richard W. Stephenson's "The Reference Facilities and Services of the Geography and Map Division, Library of Congress," published in *Proceedings of the American Congress on Surveying and Mapping, 33rd Annual Meeting, March 11–16, 1973* (p. 365–370), discusses the division's reference services in more detail.

The Geography and Map Reading Room can accommodate up to 20 researchers. On file are current editions of more than 200 cartographic, geographic, and related subject journals. Also available in the Reading Room are selected world, regional, and special subject atlases, gazetteers, globes, and more than 6,000 reference books relating principally to bibliography, cartography, geography, and history. Included in the reference collection are bound series of a number of cartographical and geographical journals. Reading Room equipment includes a microfilm-microfiche reader and a light table for use in tracing portions of maps.

A major reference tool is the Bibliography of Cartography Card File, a unique and comprehensive index to the literature of cartography. The B of C, which was originated more than 90 years ago by Philip Lee Phillips, is particularly rich in citations relating to the history of maps and cartobibliography. In 1973 the Bibliography of Cartography, comprising some 90,000 cards, was reproduced by photo-offset on permanent-durable paper in a five-volume publication by G. K. Hall and Company. References dated through 1971 are included.

The visitor to the Geography and Map Reading Room has access to some 3½ million maps and charts and more than 38,000 atlases. A dictionary card catalog gives descriptions of approximately 60 percent of the atlases, and brief notes on the remainder are included in a shelflist file. Titles of most of the Library's atlases and tables of contents for many of them are included in the seven-volume *List of Geographical Atlases in the Library of Congress,* previously cited. The two-volume *United States Atlases* lists works published between 1776 and 1950.

There is no comprehensive catalog of the division's map holdings, but several card and book catalogs provide access to specialized segments of the collection. The MARC Map catalog currently includes descriptions for more than 26,000 maps, most of which are of recent date. Some 5,000 titles are being added annually to the MARC Map storage file. Because the cartographic collections are only partially controlled through catalogs, the reading room visitor will be best served if he presents his request to one of the reference librarians. Readers are not permitted to select items personally from the map files or atlas decks.

Adjoining the Geography and Map Reading Room is a spacious (5,000 square feet) masonry vault, which has independent temperature and humidity controls. Within the vault are preserved some 6,000 rare manuscript and printed maps and more than 2,000 atlases—one of the world's finest collections of cartographic treasures and an outstanding resource for historical research in many subject fields.

All reading room patrons are asked to sign the visitors' register. Researchers who consult vault materials are also requested to complete and sign the standard "Reader's Registration Form for Use of Rare Materials." Vault items are serviced only in the rare materials alcove. The division reserves the right to substitute facsimiles or photoreproductions in the interest of preserving originals.

Four or five cartographic exhibits are mounted in the division each year, featuring pertinent selections from the division's collections of historic and current cartographic collections.

Reproductions of individual maps and plates from atlases may be ordered through the Library's Photoduplication Service, subject to copyright or other restrictions. Because of the large volume of reproduction handled by the Photoduplication Service, requesters should allow from four to six weeks for processing an order.

The Geography and Map Division has an active publications program. A list of publications in print, including bibliographies, checklists, informational brochures, exhibit catalogs, facsimiles, and reprints of articles in professional journals, is available on request. A number of the division's major cartobibliographic reference volumes, long since out of print, have in recent years been reprinted by various American and foreign commercial publishers.

☆U.S. GOVERNMENT PRINTING OFFICE: 1975 O—535—129